THE STUDENT LEADERSHIP CHALLENGE

STUDENT WORKBOOK AND
LEADERSHIP JOURNAL

FOURTH EDITION

JAMES KOUZES | BARRY POSNER

With Lisa Shannon and Bathild Junius "June" Covington

THE STUDENT LEADERSHIP CHALLENGE

STUDENT WORKBOOK AND LEADERSHIP JOURNAL

FOURTH EDITION

THE LEADERSHIP CHALLENGE®
A Wiley Brand

Published by John Wiley & Sons, Inc., Hoboken, New Jersey.
Published simultaneously in Canada.

ISBNs: 9781394279975 (paperback), 9781394279982 (ePub), 9781394279999 (ePDF)

For general information on our other products and services, please contact our Customer Care Department within the United States at (800) 762-2974, outside the United States at (317) 572- 3993. For product technical support, you can find answers to frequently asked questions or reach us via live chat at https://support.wiley.com.

If you believe you've found a mistake in this book, please bring it to our attention by emailing our reader support team at wileysupport@wiley.com with the subject line "Possible Book Errata Submission."

Wiley also publishes its books in a variety of electronic formats. Some content that appears in print may not be available in electronic formats. For more information about Wiley products, visit our web site at www.wiley.com.

Library of Congress Cataloging-in-Publication Data is Available:

ISBN 978-1-394-27997-5 (paperback)
ISBN 978-1-394-27999-9 (ePDF)
ISBN 978-1-394-27998-2 (ePUB)

Cover design: Wiley

SKY10088117_101724

Contents

Introduction

In today's world, there are countless opportunities to make a difference. More than ever before, there is a need for people of all ages, from all backgrounds, with all types of life experiences, to seize the opportunities that can lead to great success. More than ever before, there is a need for leaders to inspire people to dream, to participate, and to persevere.

The Student Leadership Challenge offers everyone the know-how to do just that: to take the initiative and make a difference. It's about mobilizing others to make extraordinary things happen—from the classroom, stadium, residence hall, Greek chapters, clubs, and student government to the campus, neighboring community, and nation. It's about the practices student leaders use to transform values into actions, visions into realities, obstacles into innovations, separateness into solidarity, and risks into rewards. It's about how students build the momentum to turn challenging opportunities into remarkable successes.

ABOUT THE STUDENT LEADERSHIP CHALLENGE

The foundation of this approach is The Five Practices of Exemplary Leadership® model. The model began with a research project in 1983 that asked people, "What did you do when you were at your 'personal best' in leading others?"

Four decades later, The Five Practices of Exemplary Leadership model continues to prove its effectiveness as a clear, evidence-based "operating system" for achieving the extraordinary. It turns the abstract concept of leadership into five easy-to-grasp practices and thirty behaviors that can be learned by anyone willing to step up and accept the challenge to lead.

In our book *The Student Leadership Challenge, Fourth Edition*, we share real-life examples and engaging stories of young people who demonstrate The Five Practices. We highly recommend you read the book to deepen your understanding of The Five Practices model. The book's examples and stories of students who demonstrate the leadership behaviors embedded in the model are intended to both inform and inspire you.

When used alongside the book, this workbook enables you to take a deep dive into your own leadership development. The activities will help you explore and deepen your understanding of each of the thirty leadership behaviors that connect to The Five Practices model. When you focus on one behavior at a time, you will identify opportunities to demonstrate that behavior more often.

An excellent way to become familiar with the thirty behaviors before you begin the activities in this workbook is by completing the Student Leadership Practices Inventory (Student LPI). When you purchase a new copy of *The Student Leadership Challenge, Fourth Edition*, instructions for accessing a complimentary Student LPI self-assessment are included. More details related to the Student LPI are discussed later in this workbook.

HOW TO USE THE STUDENT WORKBOOK AND JOURNAL

This workbook is designed to offer you a pathway for you exploring and learning about the thirty leadership behaviors that make up The Five Practices of Exemplary Leadership. We offer opportunities for you to get some practice engaging with them, reflect on your experience, and map out your ongoing leadership development journey.

Throughout the workbook, we occasionally refer to leaders of teams, groups, and organizations. We use the terms to encompass as many examples as possible. You do not need to be part of any official team, group, or organization for The Student Leadership Challenge to be relevant and useful. The concepts, ideas, and action are equally applicable for self-leadership, informal groups, and even class projects.

Getting Started introduces our point of view about leadership, reviews the origins of The Student Leadership Challenge, and provides an activity to help you identify the leader within you. It also provides an overview of The Five Practices of Exemplary Leadership model.

Next, we introduce the **Student Leadership Practices Inventory (Student LPI)**, the tool we created to measure leadership behavior. We include an overview of the assessment and guidance for using your Student LPI report with this workbook in support of your ongoing leadership development journey.

The next five sections explore each of The Five Practices in depth. We provide a summary of the practice and list of the six leadership behaviors associated with that practice from the Student LPI. The "Understand and Practice" sections provide guided activities and reflections that will help you take action to demonstrate the behaviors more frequently.

Along the way, we suggest steps to take, sometimes alone and sometimes with others, to build your skills in becoming a better leader. Whether the focus is your own learning or the development of others in your group, you can take immediate action on every one of the recommendations. They require little or no budget or approval. They just require your personal commitment and discipline.

Next, **My Leadership Journal**, is designed to support you as you take on your next leadership challenge. It walks you through the most effective form of practice: taking deliberate action, reflecting on what occurred because of your action, learning from the outcome, and taking action again.

The quotations featured in this workbook are from students in leadership classes and workshops around the world. Using their own words, they talk about the lessons they learned about leadership.

It's been said that the education and development of people is the lever to change the world, and we believe this is especially true for you as an emerging leader. In these extraordinary times, there is no shortage of challenging opportunities. But remember that all generations confront their own serious threats. The abundance of challenges is not the issue: it's how you respond to them that matters.

By improving your ability to lead, you will be better able to influence the kinds of positive changes that are needed. You will be better able to make a difference in the quality of your life and the lives of others. We know from our research that you have the capacity to learn to lead and to make extraordinary things happen. We believe in you!

1
Getting Started

Over the years we have found that students sometimes struggle to think of themselves as leaders. Some young people (and older people!) believe that leadership is a kind of magical talent that some people are born with, and others aren't. From our four decades of research, we know that is simply not true. Anyone—no matter their age, position, or title—can lead. We also know that anyone, if they choose to, can become a better leader.

Here are seven key concepts from our four decades of research that reveal what is true about leadership. We hope they will inspire you as you begin your leadership development journey.

1. **Leadership is learned.** Leadership is a process that ordinary people use when they are bringing out the best in themselves and others. It is an identifiable set of skills and abilities that is available to everyone.
2. **Leadership is a relationship.** At the heart of leadership is the ability to connect with others, understand their hopes and dreams, and engage them in pulling together for a shared dream of the future. Leaders understand that every relationship contributes to their ability to be successful.
3. **Leadership development is self-development.** Engineers have computers, painters have brushes and paints, musicians have instruments. Leaders have only themselves: that is their instrument. Committing to liberating the leader within is a personal commitment. The journey begins with an exploration of who you are from the inside out.
4. **Learning to lead is an ongoing process.** Learning to lead is a journey, not a single event or destination. You may occupy many leadership roles throughout your life. Each will deepen your understanding of what it takes to engage others and what it takes to inspire others to make extraordinary things happen with people in your life. The context in which you lead will change, and with each change comes deeper learning. The best leaders are the best learners.
5. **Leadership requires deliberate practice.** Excellence in anything—whether it's music, sports, or academics—requires deliberate practice. Leadership is no exception. You will need to devote time every day to becoming the best leader you can be.
6. **Leadership is an aspiration and a choice.** Leaders have countless chances to make a difference. If a person wants to lead others and is willing to do the work, they can lead. It is a deeply personal choice and a lifetime commitment.
7. **You make a difference.** All leadership is based on one fundamental assumption: that you matter. We have seen firsthand how a leader can make a profound difference in the lives of others. To do that, you must believe in yourself and in your capacity to have a positive influence on others. We also know that to those who are following you, you are the most important leader to them at that moment. It's not some other leader. It's you.

DEFINING LEADERSHIP

If you Google "leadership definition," you will find hundreds of different definitions of leadership. Our research that resulted in The Five Practices of Exemplary Leadership led us to the following definition:

Leadership is the art of mobilizing others to want to struggle for shared aspirations.

What words stand out to you in this definition? Circle, underline, or highlight the words that catch your attention.

Why do you think leadership is better described as an "art" versus a "science"?

Why do you think leadership is about "mobilizing others"?

What do you make of the phrase "want to struggle"? Did that part of the definition surprise you?

Describe in your own words what "shared aspirations" means.

MY PERSONAL-BEST LEADERSHIP EXPERIENCE

The research to discover what exemplary leaders do when they are at their personal best began by collecting thousands of stories from ordinary people—from students to executives in all types of organizations around the globe—about the experiences they recalled when asked to think of a peak leadership experience, that is, what they did when they were at their personal best as a leader. The collection effort continues, and the stories continue to offer compelling examples of what leaders do when making extraordinary things happen. As you begin to explore The Student Leadership Challenge and The Five Practices of Exemplary Leadership, we ask you to respond to some of the same questions asked of those involved in the original research. It's called the personal-best leadership experience, and we believe it will provide you with an inspiring view of the leader within you.

Begin by thinking about a time when you performed at your very best as a leader. A personal-best experience is an event (or a series of events) that you believe to be your individual standard of excellence. It's your own record-setting performance—a time when you achieved significant success while working with others. It is something against which you can measure yourself to determine whether you are performing as a leader at levels you know to be possible.

Your personal-best experience may have happened when you had no official authority but chose to play a leadership role within a group, organization, class project, or even a family situation. Focus on one specific experience.

Step 1

On a separate sheet of paper, describe this leadership experience by answering the following questions:

- When did it happen? How long did it last?
- What was your role? Who else was involved?
- What feelings did you have prior to and during the experience?
- Did you initiate the experience? If someone else initiated it, how did you emerge as the leader?
- What were the results of the experience?

Step 2

With relation to this experience, on a separate sheet of paper, list the actions you took as a leader that made a difference, and answer the following questions:

- What actions did you take?
- How did you get others to go beyond the ordinary levels of performance?

- What did you do to demonstrate your own commitment to the project or undertaking?
- What did you do to make sure everyone understood the purpose or goal?
- What did you or others do to overcome any major challenges or setbacks?
- What did you do to engage others and get them to participate fully?
- Based on what you did or said, what other extraordinary actions did your team or group members take?
- Summarize what you consider to be the five to seven most important actions you took as a leader who made a difference.

Step 3

Review the responses from the questions in steps 1 and 2. What three to five major lessons did you learn about leadership from this experience? (These are lessons you might share as advice to others about them being or becoming a great leader.) Write them here:

Lesson 1:

Lesson 2:

Lesson 3:

Lesson 4:

Lesson 5:

Step 4

From the lessons you identified in step 3:

What single piece of advice would you give to another individual on how to make extraordinary things happen in their organization based on your experience?

THE FIVE PRACTICES OF EXEMPLARY LEADERSHIP MODEL

To learn what people did when they were at their personal best in leading others, we interviewed hundreds of people using the same types of questions you just used to reflect on your personal-best leadership experience. The starting assumption was that asking regular people to describe extraordinary leadership experiences would reveal patterns of success.

Analyzing thousands of students' responses to the personal-best leadership experience proved that despite differences in culture, gender, or age these personal-best stories revealed similar patterns of behavior. No matter where a personal-best experience took place—whether it was in a classroom, a student club or organization, a sports team, a community service project, a part-time job, a religious or spiritual organization, or on a school field trip—when leaders were at their personal best, there were then, and are today, five core leadership practices common to all these examples: Model the Way, Inspire a Shared Vision, Challenge the Process, Enable Others to Act, and Encourage the Heart.

Model the Way

Leaders clarify values by finding their voice and affirming shared values, and they set the example by aligning actions with shared values.

The most important personal quality people look for and admire in a leader is personal credibility. Credibility is the foundation of leadership. If people don't believe in the messenger, they won't believe the message.

Leaders clarify values and establish guiding principles concerning the way people (fellow students, student groups, teachers, and advisors) should be treated and the way goals should be pursued. They create standards of excellence and then set an example for others to follow.

Titles may be granted, but leadership is earned. Leaders earn credibility by putting their values into action and living by the same standards and principles they expect of others. Leaders not only talk about the way things should be done but they also show the way they should be done.

Inspire a Shared Vision

Leaders envision the future by imagining exciting and ennobling possibilities, and they enlist others in a common vision by appealing to shared aspirations.

Leaders are driven by their clear image of possibility and what their organization could become. They passionately believe that they can make a difference. They envision the future, creating an ideal and unique image of what the group, team, or organization can be. Leaders enlist others in their dreams. They breathe life into their visions and get people to see exciting possibilities for the future.

Challenge the Process

Leaders search for opportunities by seizing the initiative and looking outward for innovative ways to improve. They experiment and take risks by constantly generating small wins and learning from experience.

Leaders are pioneers—they are willing to step out into the unknown. The work of leaders is change, and the status quo is unacceptable to them. They search for opportunities to innovate, grow, and improve. In doing so, they experiment and take risks. Because leaders know that risk-taking involves mistakes and failures, they accept the inevitable disappointments as learning opportunities. Leaders constantly ask, "What can we learn when things don't go as planned?"

Enable Others to Act

Leaders foster collaboration by building trust and facilitating relationships. They strengthen others by enhancing self-determination and developing competence.

Leaders know they can't do it alone. Leadership involves building relationships and is a group effort. Leaders foster collaboration and create spirited groups. They actively involve others. Leaders understand that they have a responsibility to bring others along. Collaboration is the master skill that enables groups, partnerships, and other alliances to function effectively. The work of leaders is making people feel strong, capable, informed, and connected.

Encourage the Heart

Leaders recognize contributions by showing appreciation for individual excellence. They celebrate the values and victories by creating a spirit of community.

Accomplishing extraordinary things in groups and organizations is hard work. The climb to the top is arduous and long; people can become exhausted, frustrated, and disenchanted. They're often tempted to give up. Genuine acts of caring uplift the spirit and draw people forward. To keep hope and determination alive, leaders recognize the contributions that individuals make. In every winning team, the members need to share in the rewards of their efforts, so leaders celebrate accomplishments. They help people feel like heroes.

Embedded within these Five Practices are thirty essential leadership behaviors that are the basis for The Student Leadership Practices Inventory (Student LPI) and are described in the next section of this workbook.

2
Your Student LPI

WHAT IS THE STUDENT LPI?

The Student Leadership Practices Inventory is a leadership development tool designed to help you measure the frequency of your leadership behaviors. The accompanying report enables you to pinpoint actions you can take to improve your effectiveness as a leader. The assessment is made up of the Student LPI Self (which you complete) and the Student LPI Observer (anonymously completed by others chosen by either you or the person administrating your Student LPI). When you purchase a new copy of *The Student Leadership Challenge, Fourth Edition*, instructions for accessing a complimentary Student LPI self-assessment are included. If you purchased a used copy and would like to purchase the LPI Self or if you would like to purchase The Student LPI 360 with Observers, please visit https://www.leadershipchallenge.com/solutions/student-leadership.aspx.

Student LPI Self

This thirty-item self-assessment measures the frequency of specific leadership behaviors on a five-point scale. It takes approximately ten to fifteen minutes to complete. It can either be used as a stand-alone self-reflection tool or in conjunction with the Student LPI Observer Assessment.

Student LPI Observer

This assessment is completed by individuals selected by you or the person administrating your assessment. It takes approximately ten to fifteen minutes to complete. Like the Student LPI Self, the Observer includes thirty items and measures the frequency of specific leadership behaviors on a five-point scale. This unique measurement tool collects valuable feedback for you from teachers, coaches, student advisors, teammates, fellow club members, coworkers, or others who have direct experience in observing you in a leadership role or any leadership capacity.

Who Is the Student LPI Designed For?

Even if you don't identify yourself as a leader, the research supporting The Student Leadership Challenge indicates that everyone has the potential to lead. The Student LPI tool was created for students with little to no formal professional experience, and it is appropriate for use in high school and college classrooms, student government, campus clubs, fraternities, sororities, first-year-experience programs, community service and service-learning organizations, athletic teams, and youth organizations. If you are looking to enhance your leadership role in your school or community, you will benefit from using the Student LPI to learn how you use The Five Practices framework and consider how you could make more use of the model as you encounter real-life challenges and opportunities.

Using Your Student LPI Report with This Workbook

The Student LPI does not measure attitudes or intentions. It focuses on actual behaviors. Your report shows how frequently you engage in each of the thirty behaviors associated with The Five Practices (six for each Practice).

It's important to recognize that the Student LPI report is not a test score or a judgment of how well you do these practices. It's a collection of observations about how often you do them and are seen doing them. As you make your way through this workbook, we encourage you to frequently revisit your report to better understand yourself and how you show up as a leader. This workbook is designed to help you practice the behaviors and to find opportunities to increase the frequency with which you engage in the leadership behaviors. The process will likely cause you to reflect on important questions:

- What behaviors come naturally to me?
- How can I build on these behaviors so that I can be a more effective leader?
- What behaviors are more difficult for me?
- How can I practice those behaviors and demonstrate them more often in a way that feels natural to my particular leadership style?

Each of the thirty behaviors from the Student LPI Self and Student LPI Observer aligns with one of The Five Practices of Exemplary Leadership. On the first page of each of the practice sections in this workbook, we list the six behaviors aligned with the practice

(**Note:** the six behaviors may be listed in a different order than how they appear in your Student LPI report). The activities that follow are designed to help you get more comfortable with those behaviors.

CAN I LEARN TO BE A BETTER LEADER?

Yes! Categorically yes. Leadership is a skill like any other skill, which means that your motivation and dedication to improve, along with feedback, practice, and good coaching, can bring improvement. However, remember that few people dramatically improve any skill overnight or in a single attempt. The Student LPI and this workbook provides a framework for you to develop routine practice opportunities. If you wanted to become good at a sport or accomplished at playing a certain instrument, you would spend time practicing. The same is true of leadership, and the Student LPI and this workbook gives you the information you need to focus your practice.

One option is to connect your Student LPI report to the Leadership Journal section in this workbook. You'll find a section in the journal that is dedicated to reflecting on your Student LPI data.

We also encourage you to share your thoughts and intentions about your Student LPI results. You might schedule a regular conversation peer-to-peer, or perhaps you can identify a mentor. Sharing this information can help you effectively plan for your personal leadership development and be accountable for the actions you identify and commit to.

The Leadership Journal provides the format for reflecting on the action you took as well and the results it produced. Over time, you can track the results of the actions, record your thinking, and return to the Student LPI. This approach aligns solidly with the premise that leadership is a skill, and you get better at it with deliberate practice.

3
Model the Way

MODEL THE WAY SUMMARY

The first step a leader must take along the path to becoming an exemplary leader is inward. It's a step toward discovering personal values and beliefs. Leaders must find their voice, determine the principles that will guide their decisions and actions, and find a way to express their leadership philosophy in their own words.

Leaders don't speak just for themselves. They are often the voice for their team, their group, or their organization. Leadership is a dialogue, not a monologue. Therefore, they must reach out to others. They must understand and appreciate the values of their constituents and find a way to affirm shared values. Leaders *forge* unity. They don't *force* it. They give people reasons to care, not orders to follow.

Leaders stand up for their beliefs. They practice what they preach. Their actions demonstrate to others the values they profess. They also ensure that others adhere to the values that have been agreed on. It is consistency between words and actions that build credibility.

This deep understanding of self and a consistency of word and deed makes Model the Way the bedrock from which leaders can effectively engage in the other practices of exemplary leadership.

MODEL THE WAY BEHAVIORS

- I talk about my values and the principles that guide my actions.
- I set a personal example of what I expect from other people.
- I follow through on the promises and commitments I make.
- I seek to understand how my actions affect other people's performance.
- I spend time making sure that people behave consistently with the principles and standards we have agreed on.
- I make sure that people support the values we have agreed on.

"To know how to lead, you need to know where you are going. To know where you are going, you have to know who you are. Knowing yourself truly means that you have to be honest with yourself."

—Tommy Baldacci

UNDERSTAND AND PRACTICE THE LEADERSHIP BEHAVIORS OF MODEL THE WAY

I talk about my values and the principles that guide my actions.

MODEL THE WAY

This activity helps you clarify or shine a light on your personal values. It also helps you understand the wide range of values people hold and the notion that there is no one right set of values.

Step 1. From the list of values on page 23, underline your top ten values.

Step 2. From your list of ten, circle your top five values.

Step 3. List your five most important values in the following space. Take a few minutes to think about these values and define them. Describe what they meant to you. Jot down your notes next to each value.

Step 4. Answer the additional questions at the bottom of the page.

My Five Most Important Values and Their Definitions

1.

2.

3.

4.

5.

Recall a moment or situation in the past that influenced your most important values choices. Reflect on how this personal history has determined *why* you chose one or more of your values.

How do your values align or conflict with your family's values? How about the school you attend or a group that you belong to?

Values List

Achievement	Family time	Patience
Autonomy	Flexibility	Power
Beauty	Freedom	Productivity
Caring	Friendship	Profitability
Caution	Fun	Prosperity and wealth
Challenge	Growth	Quality
Communication	Happiness	Recognition
Competence	Harmony	Responsibility
Competition	Health	Risk-taking
Courage	Honesty and integrity	Security
Cooperation	Hope	Service to others
Creativity	Human relationships	Simplicity
Curiosity	Humor	Speed
Customer focus	Independence	Spirituality and faith
Decisiveness	Individualism	Strength
Dependability	Innovation	Success
Determination	Intelligence	Task focus
Discipline	Involvement	Teamwork
Diversity	Learning	Trust
Effectiveness	Love and affection	Truth
Empathy	Loyalty	Uniqueness
Equality	Open-mindedness	Variety
Fairness	Organization	Winning
Family	Respect	Wisdom

Find three people with whom you feel you can talk about your values. Ask them if they knew these were things you stood for before you told them. If they reply yes, ask them how they knew. If they reply no, ask them what they perceive *is* important to you and why they believe that.

Name	They Know What I Value	Yes/How or No/Why Not?

As you talk about your values, does your language or meaning for them change the more you describe them to others? If so, how? Capture your refined definitions as you get more clarity on what they mean to you.

Additional notes and observations on values:

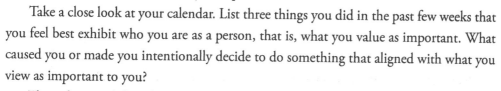

I set a personal example of what I expect from other people.

How you spend your time is the single clearest indicator of what's important to you. People use this metric to judge whether you measure up to the standard you set. Spending time on what you say is important shows that you are true to your values. It is also a highly visible indicator of what you expect from others.

Take a close look at your calendar. List three things you did in the past few weeks that you feel best exhibit who you are as a person, that is, what you value as important. What caused you or made you intentionally decide to do something that aligned with what you view as important to you?

Three things I did in the past few weeks that were aligned with what I value:

I know the first action was aligned with my values because (What is it about your actions that demonstrates your values?):

1.

2.

3.

I know the second action was aligned with my values because (What is it about your actions that demonstrate your values?):

I know the third action was aligned with my values because (What is it about your actions that demonstrates your values?):

Considering the three items you listed. Write a sentence or two about the positive impact you have on other people when your actions align with what you believe to be important.

Ask any of the people with whom you've been talking about your values for examples of when they have seen you living out those values. Also ask for examples of times when they have heard you say or do things that are not in line with your values. Define an action you can take to continue or better live your values based on what you have learned.

Values Conversations Notes

Value	Yes/How?	No/They Saw

Think about the activities that might not show up on your calendar. Are you spending time on things that *do not* align with what you believe to be important? List here and reflect on how your actions affect those around you and how you might change how you spend your time in the future.

MODEL THE WAY

I follow through on the promises and commitments I make.

What are three recent promises you made to someone else? Did you keep them (follow through on them)? If so, describe how. If not, describe why you didn't keep your promise. In either case, what impact did this have on your credibility with and relationship to others?

Promise	Kept	Didn't Keep	Why/Impact
1.			
2.			
3.			

Make a list of three commitments you have made to others in the past five days. Next to each item, write why you made that commitment. Next to that, write how much time (and any other relevant resources) you think the commitment will take (or did, if you fulfilled it).

Commitment	Reason for Commitment	Time/Resources Required
1.		
2.		
3.		

When was the last time you made a commitment that you wish you had not? What was it? Did this commitment align with your goals? What about this experience detracted from your doing something more valuable? What else could you have done with this time that would have made a better impact?

Commitment I would take back:

Why:

A better use of my time would have been:

Think about a commitment or promise that you haven't followed through on. Write an action that you will take in the next forty-eight to seventy-two hours to work toward meeting that promise.

Commitment I did not follow through on:

To meet my commitment, in the next forty-eight to seventy-two hours I will:

Think of the last time that you said no to a request, a group invitation, or something that involved an investment of your time. How did this make you feel? Did you feel emotions of missing out, or did you feel liberated by your decision?

MODEL THE WAY

I seek to understand how my actions affect other people's performance.

Describe the last time you asked someone for any type of feedback about something specific you did. What did you do with that information? How did it feel?

Feedback requested from:

Feedback was for:

The feedback I got was:

My reaction:

How I used this feedback:

What strong feelings, positive or negative, have you had in response to feedback that you have received? Why did you have that reaction? Was there anything in the feedback that you felt was accurate or productive even if you didn't respond positively to it?

Positive feelings:

Negative feelings:

Overall reaction (how I behaved in response to the feedback):

Useful lessons I took away from the feedback:

Describe a time when you received feedback about something others thought you did really well. How have you or will you use that information to help repeat those or similar actions in the future?

Encouraging feedback I received:

To make this information useful, I will:

Who are three people you work with (at a job or as part of a team or in group participate in) that you could ask for feedback? Schedule a time to ask them for feedback on your work. From the comments you receive, write down what you think the main themes are about how others describe your work. Define a specific action step to take for one thing you want to repeat and one thing you want to work on and improve. As you begin to take action on these two items, revisit your list of themes and select two more on which you can focus.

Comment	Theme	Action Step: Repeat	Action Step: Improve

As you begin to take action on these two items, revisit your list of themes and select two more on which you can focus.

I spend time making sure that people behave consistently with the principles and standards we have agreed on.

List the principles and standards of a team, group, or organization that you belong to. Sometimes these are formally discussed and agreed on; however, quite often they are more casually presumed. For example, a soccer coach might discuss with their team what should happen if players miss a practice and everyone then agrees that missing practice means you don't start the next game. Or, at your part-time job, you begin to notice that during meetings, everyone is encouraged to speak up before a decision is made. While it's not a formal policy, you can tell that everyone has bought into the idea that every employee has a voice that should be listened to and respected.

Group values:

From the list of values, name a time when you have talked about any of these and with whom:

I talked with ____________________ on __________________ about the following values:

How do you both think you can live up to the values as individuals?

How do you both think the group lives up to the values?

What does it look like when the group doesn't live up to the values?

Together write an action you can share and take with the group to work toward living up to the values of the group:

How did this discussion go? Was it easy, hard, comfortable, or uncomfortable for you? What about for the other person? What did you learn about how you expressed your values to someone else?

I make sure that people support the values we have agreed on.

Watch this YouTube video about SPANX founder Sarah Blakely: https://www.youtube.com/watch?v=_TeV9op6Mp8.

Or, you can Google "Sara Blakely dinner with dad" to find other videos with the same story.

What value did Sara Blakely's father instill in his kids?

How did he make sure his children lived up to that value?

How did his repeated dinner time conversation affect Sara's behavior as she grew up?

"I had to lead by example. I had to be the doer, not the preacher. I realize that people are constantly observing us. When they see your actions are in sync with your words, you are a more effective leader. And perhaps that is why it was only when I did those things myself that my roommates followed."

—Della Dsouza

FURTHER ACTIONS FOR INCREASING THE FREQUENCY OF MODEL THE WAY BEHAVIORS

Leadership development is an ongoing process. To continue on the path to becoming a better leader, try out one or more of the activities listed here:

1. At the beginning of each day, reflect about what you want to achieve for that day. Think in terms of what you know is important to you and what in your schedule contributes to that importance. You might ask yourself, "How do I want to show up as a leader today?" At the end of the day, reflect on what happened. What did you do as a leader that you are most proud of? Where were the opportunities that you missed that you could take advantage of another day? Can you do anything tomorrow about those opportunities? What other actions can you take tomorrow that show you can lead better?
2. If you are in a group and have a formal, defined leadership role, see how you can work directly with or shadow someone else in the group. In essence, trade places with that person and work on something together. Use this as an opportunity to get feedback from others as to what you are doing related to their work in the group.
3. Use a planner, smartphone, journal, note app, or some other resource to regularly write notes to yourself about the commitments and promises you are making to yourself and others. Write the dates on which you have committed to fulfilling them and check regularly on your progress.
4. Keep track of how you spend your time. What is important to you and what you value often show up in how you spend your time and prioritize what you do every day and over the course of weeks and months. Look to see if you are investing large amounts of your time in things that are not that important to you or that you really don't value. The same might also be said about people and relationships. What can you do to adjust your schedule so that you are aligning your actions more with your values?
5. Search out and study other leaders who live out their values. How do their stated values show up in their actions and what they consistently say?

CONNECT WHAT YOU LEARNED ABOUT MODEL THE WAY TO YOUR PERSONAL LEADERSHIP JOURNAL

The Leadership Journal is available on page 101 to help you shape your ongoing learning. After working through this Model the Way section of the workbook and reviewing your Student Leadership Practices Inventory, we invite you to capture some highlights of what you learned and consider your next steps. Use the journal section as a support tool for tackling your next leadership challenge.

4

Inspire a Shared Vision

INSPIRE A SHARED VISION SUMMARY

Leaders look toward the future with a vision of what could be or what could be better. They imagine what is possible if everyone works together for a common purpose. They are positive about the future and passionately believe that people can make a difference.

But visions are insufficient to generate organized movement. Other people must experience the excitement of future possibilities. Leaders breathe life into visions. They communicate hopes and dreams so that others clearly understand and share them as their own.

As leaders start to imagine the possibilities, they must visualize the details: what this image of the future looks, feels, and sounds like. They must paint a picture of it until it looks so real that they can articulate it with passion and conviction. Leaders are expressive, and they attract followers through their energy, optimism, and hope. With strong appeals and quiet persuasion, they develop enthusiastic supporters.

The Five Practices of Exemplary Leadership build on each other. When leaders Model the Way, they have a clearly defined set of values and encourage those in their group to also define the values they will share and live by. Leaders strive to align their actions with the values they hold. They also guide the group to act based on clearly identified shared values. A logical progression from this values-based foundation is to then envision how things could be better. This is the heart of Inspire a Shared Vision. Leaders offer their image of the future to others as an invitation to join together and pursue a better place, while taking into consideration others' dreams and aspirations.

INSPIRE A SHARED VISION BEHAVIORS

- I look ahead and communicate about what I believe will affect us in the future.
- I am upbeat and positive when talking about what we can accomplish.
- I talk with others about a vision of how things could be even better in the future.
- I speak with passion about the higher purpose and meaning of what we are doing.
- I talk with others about how their own interests can be met by working toward a common goal.
- I describe to others in our organization what we should be capable of accomplishing.

"The more I saw what was possible, the more I became excited."

—Divya Pari

UNDERSTAND AND PRACTICE INSPIRE A SHARED VISION

I look ahead and communicate about what I believe will affect us in the future.

Come Join Me on Vacation Activity

This activity helps you practice engaging others with your vision of the future. The notion of creating a compelling vision that inspires and drives people to action can seem daunting. However, like anything else you want to master, it simply takes practice. This exercise helps you see that you already have the basic skills of looking ahead, imagining an exciting future, and passionately sharing that vision in a way that personally connects with the people you'd like to join you.

After completing this exercise, you will see how a vision begins from your own values and passion and then connects to the values and passions of others.

1. Think about a place where you have gone on vacation and would love to return to with your friends.
2. Close your eyes and think about this place. What do you feel, hear, taste, or smell? What makes you want to smile? Open your eyes and take some short notes about what you experienced.
3. Ask one or more of your close friends to let you practice your visioning technique with them. Invite each friend to spend time with you at this vacation place. Without naming the location, describe it (use your feel, hear, taste, and smell notes). Think about the kinds of vacations the friend you are talking with prefers. What do they like to do? How do they like to spend their free time? Using your own enthusiasm and your personal insight, invite them in a way that will inspire them to join you and spend time in this place with you.

Notes on Your Place

Notes on Your Experience of Inviting Your Friends

INSPIRE A SHARED VISION

I am upbeat and positive when talking about what we can accomplish.

I talk with others about a vision of how things could be even better in the future.

What is your issue or cause? How can you articulate your vision (large or small—saving the polar bears or winning a basketball game) and then breathing life into that vision with your words so that we can enlist others by appealing to shared aspirations. We can do this through one or more techniques:

- Symbolic language
- Images of the future
- Appealing to the common good
- Positive communication
- Expressing emotions
- Speaking genuinely, in my own words

Create a short two- to three-minute "elevator speech" for your vision using these techniques. After you have found the right words, deliver your speech in front of a mirror several times. Fine-tune it.

My Vision

I used these techniques
___ Symbolic language
___ Images of the future
___ Appealing to the common good
___ Positive communication
___ Expressing emotions
___Speaking genuinely, in my own words

Memorize your elevator speech. Practice saying it in front of your friends and ask for feedback. Are you upbeat and positive? Are you clear about what can be accomplished when working together? Record feedback here:

INSPIRE A SHARED VISION

I speak with passion about the higher purpose and meaning of what we are doing.

These short videos will help you think about and articulate your particular higher purpose and get better at communicating it.

First, watch this Simon Sinek video "What a Vision Is" (Find this video on YouTube by searching "Simon Sinek What a Vision Is" or by going to this URL: https://www.youtube.com/watch?v=Kqlx29Kuyig.)

Now look back at your elevator speech on the previous page. When you have practiced sharing it with friends, did it feel like revealing the tip of the iceberg, as Simon Sinek describes? What ways can you get better at showing with your words what can't be seen today?

This video is an example of a very young person who successfully started a movement. Watch Greta Thunberg speaking in front of European Union leaders. (Find this video on YouTube by searching "Greta Thunberg's Emotional Speech to EU leaders" or by going to this URL: https://www.youtube.com/watch?v=FWsM9-_zrKo.)

What did you notice about how Greta spoke about higher purpose? What techniques did she use to connect with and appeal to her audience?

Which of these techniques can you use to improve your elevator speech? How will you implement them?

> I talk with others about how their own interests can be met by working toward a common goal.

On a scale of 1 to 10, think about what you know about other members of a group or team that you belong to. How well do you know what they hope to gain from being in the group or team? Circle the number on the number line. Given this score, what are ways you can engage more with everyone or with the few whom you might not know well?

I know what members of the group hope to gain from being in the group:

Not Very Well | Very Well

Name	1	2	3	4	5	6	7	8	9	10

Here are some actions I can take to move my score more toward a 10.

What would you specifically ask others in order to learn about their goals and reasons for being in the group? What questions will help you learn about the vision they have for themselves while in the organization? What questions would help you understand their vision for the group as a whole?

I will ask the following questions of the group members to get to know their reasons for being a member of this group:

-
-
-

To better understand what the members of the group hope to accomplish and how they hope to grow by being a member of this group, I will ask the following questions:

-
-
-

To better understand what vision the group members have for the group itself, I will ask the following questions:

-
-
-

In your next meeting with an organization in which you're involved, spend a few minutes listening to what people in the group say is important to them. Summarize what you learned from listening to them:

On this date,________________, I spoke with the group to learn more about what is important to the members in terms of their involvement in the group. In this conversation, I learned:

INSPIRE A SHARED VISION

I describe to others in our organization what we should be capable of accomplishing.

When was the last time you spoke to a group you're leading about what you envision it doing in the future? What specifically did you say about what you envision?

We discussed our future as a group on ____________ and the vision I/we described was:

Describe the concept of "ideal." If you had a vision for a group you are leading that was "ideal," what would that mean to you? How close to ideal is your vision for the group?

If the group were an ideal or model group of its kind, it would be:

At this point, I would say our group is ____________ percent of the ideal group it needs to be.

If you haven't had a conversation with this group in which you talk about what it is capable of, list three to five things you think the group can do to make a difference. How will you describe these possibilities to the members? Write out a statement that will help you express what you believe the possibilities to be.

This group can make a greater difference if it focused on doing these things:

-
-
-
-

> "Being a leader often means going out on a ledge; it means being scared sometimes. But you shouldn't be afraid to see things differently because sometimes your perspective is the one that is necessary and enables you to lead."
>
> —Kirstyn Cole

FURTHER ACTIONS FOR INCREASING THE FREQUENCY OF INSPIRE A SHARED VISION BEHAVIORS

Leadership development is an ongoing process. To continue on the path to becoming a better leader, try out one or more of the activities listed here:

1. Who are other leaders you find inspiring? Study and read about them to see how they communicate their vision for those they lead. What is it about what and how they say things that stands out to you and is the reason for your inspiration? Think about how you can learn from what they say and do.
2. Watch or listen to Dr. Martin Luther King Jr.'s "I Have a Dream" speech. How does Dr. King Inspire a Shared Vision? What techniques does he use to capture the hearts and minds of his audience?
3. Think about how you can stay aware of future trends. Make a list of websites you can visit. Podcasts you can listen to. Books and magazines you can read.
4. Join a local Toastmasters group to gain the skills needed for communicating an inspiring vision of the future. Find more information at www.toastmasters.org.
5. Picture yourself in five years. What will you be doing and with whom? Spend some time thinking about your ideal future.

CONNECT WHAT YOU LEARNED ABOUT INSPIRE A SHARED VISION TO YOUR PERSONAL LEADERSHIP JOURNAL

The Leadership Journal is available on page 101 to help you shape your ongoing learning. After working through this Inspire a Shared Vision section of the workbook and reviewing your Student Leadership Practices Inventory, we invite you to capture some highlights of what you learned and consider your next steps. Use the journal section as a support tool for tackling your next leadership challenge.

5

Challenge the Process

CHALLENGE THE PROCESS SUMMARY

Challenge provides the opportunity for greatness. People perform at their best when there's a chance to make a significant change or improvement. Maintaining the status quo simply breeds mediocrity. Leaders seek and accept challenging opportunities to test their abilities. They motivate others to exceed their self-perceived limits and seize the initiative to make something meaningful happen. Leaders treat every assignment as an adventure.

Most innovations are not initiated by the leaders themselves, but from the people closest to the work. Innovations also germinate from "outsight"—the way exemplary leaders look outward for good ideas. Leaders promote external communication and then listen, take advice, and learn.

Progress is made incrementally, not in giant leaps. Exemplary leaders move forward in small steps with little victories. They turn adversity into advantage and setbacks into successes. They persevere with grit and determination.

Leaders venture out. They test and they take risks with bold ideas. And because risk-taking involves mistakes and failure, leaders accept and grow from the inevitable disappointments. They treat these as opportunities to learn and grow.

CHALLENGE THE PROCESS BEHAVIORS

- I look for ways to develop and challenge my skills and abilities.
- I take initiative in experimenting with the way things can be done.
- I search for innovative ways to improve what we are doing.
- I make sure that big projects we undertake are broken down into smaller and doable parts.
- I look for ways that others can try out new ideas and methods.
- When things don't go as we expected, I ask, "What can we learn from this experience?"

> "A big question I always like to ask myself is, If not me, then who? If I'm not going to do the work, then who will?"
>
> —Ceena Vang

UNDERSTAND AND PRACTICE THE LEADERSHIP BEHAVIORS OF CHALLENGE THE PROCESS

CHALLENGE THE PROCESS

I look for way to develop and challenge my skills and abilities.

What are three strengths, skills, or abilities you want to learn or develop that would help you be a better leader?

Think about a leader you admire. This could be a public figure, industry leader, or leaders within an organization you belong to. What are the leadership strengths, skills, and abilities they exhibit?

There is no right or wrong definition of leadership strengths, skills, and abilities here; simply think about what you admire about them that contributes to their strength and success as a leader.

Here are some ideas that you may have read about in *The Student Leadership Challenge*:

- Listen to and Promote Diverse Perspectives [p. 142]
- Generate Small Wins [p. 152]
- Learn from Experience [p. 161]

Pick three leadership strengths from the leader you admire and list them here:

1.

2.

3.

Why did you choose these strengths?

How do you think these strengths could affect your leadership style?

In this process, did you discover a strength, skill, or ability that you hadn't considered but now think is important?

How are some ways you can develop these strengths, skills, and abilities?

I take initiative in experimenting with the way things can be done.

To expand your experience in experimenting with the way things can be done, think about where you can find opportunities and who might be best to help you with those.

Where can you find a group, activity, or project that offers opportunities to learn new skills or enhance your existing ones? In thinking about a possible group, activity, or project, is there something that has caught your attention or made you curious? That might be a great place to start.

Whom do you know who has the skills you want to develop?

Can you talk to that person to learn from their experiences?

How did they develop those skills and talents?

Whom do you know who can provide you with feedback on your current level of relevant leadership skills and abilities?

How will you evaluate your progress in developing your skills?

I search for innovative ways to improve what we are doing.

CHALLENGE THE PROCESS

Apollo 13 (1995) Movie Activity

In this film, the spacecraft *Apollo 13* suffers a massive explosion while on its way to the moon in a section of the craft where the oxygen tanks are located that puts the lives of the three astronauts at risk: James A. Lovell Jr., the commander; John L. Swigert Jr., the command module pilot; and Fred W. Haise Jr., the lunar module pilot. For nearly six days, the ship and its crew are handicapped by the explosion and are without a plan to return to Earth safely. The NASA space program is still young and has never before encountered the situation.

Watch these clips from the movie:

"Failure Is Not an Option": https://www.youtube.com/watch?v=TA8SXpyg4O4
"Square Peg in a Round Hole": https://www.youtube.com/watch?v=ry55--J4_VQ

When you have finished watching the clips, ask yourself the following related questions:

Both Scenes:

What risks were apparent in both of these situations, and how did the teams and individuals address them?

How might past experiences have influenced the work either group was doing?

"Failure Is Not an Option" Scene:

What did you see happening in the conversation with the NASA director before the team develops a solution?

What did Gene Krantz (the mission control flight director) do to help the team craft a solution?

How do you think Krantz's interaction made the team feel? How might that have affected their performance?

What are the team's first steps in working to find a solution?

I make sure that big projects we undertake are broken down into smaller and doable parts.

CHALLENGE THE PROCESS

Breaking Down a Project and Setting Milestones Activity

Think about a large group project that you are involved with. What are three components for which you can establish milestones with your group to meet in the upcoming time frames that are most appropriate for your project? Describe the time frames for each portion of the project that best suit your group's meeting and work schedules.

Week

1.

2.

3.

Month

1.

2.

3.

Quarter/Semester

1.

2.

3.

How will you help your group determine if these milestones were met?

If you do meet them, do you know what actions contributed to your success?

If you don't meet them, do you know what factors prevented success?

CHALLENGE THE PROCESS

I look for ways that others can try out new ideas and methods.

To explore ways that others can try out new ideas and methods, organize a "meet and eat" series. A working title could be "Greet Innovation!" but you can always explore ideas for what you would want to call the series.

Here is a proposed structure for "Greet Innovation!" to provide a platform where students can experiment with new ideas and methods, fostering creativity and innovation. Plan a series of meet and eats, each focusing on a different topic or skill. For example:

- Week 1. Brainstorming techniques. To help elevate cognitive function and mood, possible snacks could be a variety of trail mixes and dark chocolate.
- Week 2. Prototyping and design thinking. Possible snacks could be fruit and vegetable platters that are colorful and appealing. Another option could be a DIY snack bar with build-your-own-yogurt parfaits or nacho stations.
- Week 3. Digital tools for innovation. To help keep participants engaged (caffeinated!) you could set up a coffee and tea bar with a variety of flavors and add-ins. Small "byte-sized" sandwiches or cookies shaped like gadgets would be fun and playful.
- Week 4. Pitching and presenting new ideas. To add an air of formality you could provide elegant hors d'oeuvres, and fancy and festive nonalcoholic mocktails. Keep in mind for all these meet and eats there will need to be options for people who are vegetarian or vegan and who have food allergies.

If you are interested in modifying and creating your own version of this idea, follow these steps to implement the series:

1. Form a planning committee. Recruit a diverse group of students to help plan and organize the meet and eat series.
2. Identify key areas of interest. Conduct a survey or brainstorming session to identify topics or areas where students are interested in innovating (e.g., technology, arts, sustainability, community service).
3. Invite guest speakers and facilitators. Bring in experts from various fields to share their experiences and conduct hands-on activities.
4. Encourage participation and collaboration. Create an open and inclusive environment where students feel comfortable sharing their ideas. Form small groups to work on mini-projects during each meet and eat.
5. Provide resources and support. Offer materials, tools, and resources necessary for experimentation (e.g., software, craft supplies, access to labs).
6. Showcase and reflect. At the end of the series, organize a showcase event where students can present their projects and reflect on their learning experiences. Provide a platform for feedback and discussion on what worked, what didn't, and potential improvements.

Example milestones:

Week

- Form planning committee and identify areas of interest.
- Develop meet and eat schedules and invite speakers.
- Promote the series and open registration.

Month

- Conduct the first set of meet and eats.
- Gather feedback and adjust the following sessions based on participant input.

Quarter/Semester

- Complete the meet and eat series.
- Host a showcase event.
- Evaluate the series and plan for future iterations.

Evaluation

- Feedback surveys. Collect feedback from participants after each meet and eat.
- Participation metrics. Track attendance and engagement levels.
- Project outcomes. Assess the quality and creativity of the projects developed during the series.
- Reflection sessions. Hold debrief sessions with the planning committee to discuss successes and areas for improvement.

By organizing the "Greet Innovation" meet and eat, students can actively look for ways to try out new ideas and methods, encouraging a culture of continuous learning and experimentation.

CHALLENGE THE PROCESS

When things don't go as we expected, I ask, "What can we learn from this experience?"

What experience did you recently have that didn't go as you expected?

What are one, two, or three specific things you learned from this experience that will benefit you in the future?

1.

2.

3.

For each item you just identified, write down how you can use what you learned when you have another opportunity to experiment.

1.

2.

3.

What are some ways you have come to think about mistakes that have made you resilient?

How can you share your own experiences with mistakes and learn from them with others you work with?

> "New things are challenging and exciting, and it takes going out of your comfort zone to see that."
>
> —Courtney Ballagh

FURTHER ACTIONS FOR INCREASING THE FREQUENCY OF CHALLENGE THE PROCESS BEHAVIORS

Leadership development is an ongoing process. To continue on the path to becoming a better leader, try out one or more of the activities listed here:

1. Make a list of tasks that you perform that are related to your various leadership activities. For each task, ask yourself, "Why am I doing this? Why am I doing it this way? Can this task be eliminated or done significantly better?" Based on your responses, do you see where you can develop other skills? Identify those skills and look for applicable opportunities within your leadership activities where you can work to develop the skills you have identified.
2. Make a list of the things your group does that are basically done the same way as they have always been done before. For each routine, ask, "Are we doing this at our best?" If yes, then carry on! If no, look for ways to change to make it better.
3. Ask others in your group what frustrates them about the organization. Make a commitment to change three of the most frequently mentioned items that are frustrating people and probably hindering the group's success.
4. Call or visit your counterparts in other organizations at your school, another school or group, or another community (both those in groups similar to yours and different from yours). Find out what they are doing and learn from their successes and challenges. Copy what they do well and use their failures as a guide for improvement.
5. Eliminate the phrase "That's the way we did it last year" from all discussions. Use the results of past programs or projects to learn from, but don't fall into the trap of doing something the same way simply because it's easier.

CONNECT WHAT YOU LEARNED ABOUT CHALLENGE THE PROCESS TO YOUR LEADERSHIP JOURNAL

The Leadership Journal is available on page 101 to help you shape your ongoing learning. After working through this Challenge the Process section of the workbook and reviewing your Student Leadership Practices Inventory, we invite you capture some highlights of what you learned and consider your next steps. Use the journal section as a support tool for tackling your next leadership challenge.

6
Enable Others to Act

ENABLE OTHER TO ACT SUMMARY

Leaders know they cannot achieve great success alone. They need partners to make extraordinary things happen in teams, small groups, or larger organizations. Exemplary student leaders create an atmosphere of mutual respect and trust, nurturing an atmosphere where people can rely on each other while working hard together. They build connected groups where people take ownership of the group's success.

Building teamwork starts with establishing and sustaining trust. It also requires clear cooperative goals based on shared values and vision. Leaders understand that being trustworthy is the reciprocal of trusting others and focus on *we*, not *I*.

Leaders see power as an expandable resource and strive to make each person feel empowered, essentially turning followers into leaders. Great leaders, in other words, create more leaders.

Leaders understand that strengthening others begins with them. They allow others to grow by letting them handle critical tasks and choose how to tackle them. Leaders ensure individual efforts are visible and recognized, and they facilitate connections for support.

ENABLE OTHERS TO ACT BEHAVIORS

- I treat others with dignity and respect.
- I actively listen to diverse points of view.
- I provide opportunities for others to take on leadership responsibilities.
- I give others a great deal of freedom and choice in deciding how to do their work.
- I foster cooperative rather than competitive relationships among the people I work with.
- I support the decisions that other people make on their own.

"The achievement of dreams and ambitions is rarely the product of contributions of a single person. Exemplary leaders enlist the help of others and build a team to embark upon the path that achieves mutual success. However, people can only apply themselves to the greatest extent when mutual trust between themselves and the leader is evident."

—Stephanie Sorg

UNDERSTAND AND PRACTICE THE LEADERSHIP BEHAVIORS OF ENABLE OTHERS TO ACT

I treat others with dignity and respect.

Watch "How You Treat People Is Who You Are" on YouTube: https://youtu.be/7dVeiYI79fQ.

Reflect on the key message of the video. Answer the following questions:

- What does the phrase "How you treat people is who you are" mean to you?

- Recall a recent interaction when you felt you treated someone well. What actions did you take, and how did it make you feel?

- Recall a recent interaction when you felt you could have treated someone better. What actions did you take, and what would you do differently now?

ENABLE OTHERS TO ACT

I actively listen to diverse points of view.

What does active listening mean to you?

Define active listening.

Active listening helps promote trust. Evaluate your own level of trust in leaders you have known. Think about two people in leadership positions or roles—one you trust and one you do not trust. They do not have to be from a current situation.

Trust	Lack of Trust
List the traits or behaviors you believe helped you trust this person.	List the traits or behaviors you believe led you to not trust this person.

Trust	Lack of Trust
What impact did this person's behavior have on you and your work?	What impact did this person's behavior have on you and your work?

ENABLE OTHERS TO ACT

I provide opportunities for others to take on leadership responsibilities.

Write your answers to the following questions:

- Why is it important to provide leadership opportunities to others?

- How can I delegate more leadership tasks that will benefit both the individual and the organization?

Write down a list of tasks or projects that need to be completed. Include a mix of both simple and complex tasks to provide a range of leadership opportunities.

For each task or project, consider the following:

- What skills and qualities are needed to lead this task?

- How can this task help someone develop their leadership skills?

List two people in your team or organization who could benefit from a leadership opportunity. Consider their current roles, strengths, and areas for growth.

Person	Current Roles	Strengths	Areas for Growth
1.			
2.			

Think of current tasks and projects for which you see a need for leadership. Match each task or project with one or both people based on their skills and development needs.

Task/Project	Person	Skills	Development Needs

Write down one specific action you will take in the next month to provide a leadership opportunity for each person.

I give others a great deal of freedom and choice in deciding how to do their work.

Describe your current approach to leadership.

- How much freedom and choice do you typically give others in deciding how to do their work?

- Can you recall specific instances when you provided significant autonomy to team members?

- What was the outcome?

- How do you feel about relinquishing control over how tasks are performed?

Rate yourself on a scale of 1 (Never) to 5 (Always) on your ability to enable others to act:

	1	2	3	4	5
I trust my team members to make decisions about their work.					
I encourage team members to find their own solutions to problems.					
I provide clear goals and expectations but allow flexibility in how they are achieved.					
I support team members in taking initiative and experimenting with new approaches.					
I refrain from micromanaging and allow team members to manage their own tasks.					

Based on your responses to the "your ability to enable others to act" evaluation, write down specific actions you will take to better enable others to act in the future.

ENABLE OTHERS TO ACT

I foster cooperative rather than competitive relationships among the people I work with.

- What does a cooperative work environment mean to you? Why is it important in the workplace?

- How can competition negatively affect team dynamics?

Reflect on your own behavior and tendencies.

- Do you tend to encourage more cooperative or competitive behaviors among your colleagues?

- Can you recall a time when you successfully fostered cooperation? What was the outcome?

- Can you recall a time when competition caused issues in your team? How was it resolved?

- What new and specific actions will you take to foster cooperative relationships in your workplace?

I support the decisions that other people make on their own.

- What does it mean to you to support someone else's decision?

- How do you think supporting others' decisions can benefit the team and the individual?

Reflect on your own behavior and tendencies.

- When do you find it challenging to support decisions made by others without your input?

- Think of a time that you successfully supported someone else's decision? What was the outcome?

- Describe a time when you struggled to support someone else's decision. What happened, and what could you have done differently?

> "Once athletes began showing more support toward one another, I was able to get them to buy in to the larger idea that fostering collaboration and sharing growth is in everyone's best interest."
>
> —Zachary Chien

FURTHER ACTIONS TO IMPROVE ENABLE OTHERS TO ACT

Leadership development is an ongoing process. To continue on the path to becoming a better leader, try out one or more of the activities listed here:

1. Encourage others to take on important tasks or projects. Suggest names of people in the group who are well-suited for a particular project. Talk to them about taking on responsibilities, expressing your confidence in their abilities and judgment.
2. Give up a regular task, not just one you don't want to do, but one that someone else in the group could benefit from taking on. Explain that this is an opportunity for them to grow and develop, not just you offloading a task.
3. Improve relationships and develop trust by doing something together outside regular group activities. Find ways to interact informally to build stronger bonds.
4. For the next two weeks, try to replace *I* with *we* when leading a group. Emphasize that leadership is about the team, not just one individual. Instead of saying, "*I'm* going to . . . ," say, "*We* can do this. . . ."

CONNECT WHAT YOU LEARNED ABOUT ENABLE OTHERS TO ACT TO YOUR LEADERSHIP JOURNAL

The Leadership Journal is available on page 101 to help you shape your ongoing learning. After working through this Enable Others to Act section of the workbook and reviewing your Student Leadership Practices Inventory, we invite you capture some highlights of what you learned and consider your next steps. Use the journal section as a support tool for tackling your next leadership challenge.

7

Encourage the Heart

ENCOURAGE THE HEART SUMMARY

Achieving extraordinary results in organizations is challenging. The journey is typically long, difficult, and demanding. Leaders inspire others to keep going by staying positive and offering motivating feedback that can help energize and refocus their team.

Leaders set standards for themselves and their teams that can inspire and elevate how everyone contributes. They provide clear direction, strong encouragement, personal attention, and meaningful feedback. They let people know that they are winners, and winners are motivated to keep improving. Leaders recognize and celebrate people's contributions, expressing pride in their accomplishments and letting them know they are heroes.

Celebrating group achievements adds fun to hard work and strengthens team spirit. Celebrations build connections and promote information sharing. Strong interpersonal relationships enhance productivity and improve both physical and psychological well-being.

ENCOURAGE THE HEART BEHAVIORS

- I encourage others as they work on activities and programs.
- I express appreciation for the contributions people make.
- I make sure that people are creatively recognized for their contributions.
- I praise people for a job well done.
- I make it a point to publicly recognize people who show commitment to shared values.
- I find ways for us to celebrate accomplishments.

> "Recognition makes a difference: whether it is for a six-year-old who just beat their first time or a senior swimmer who hasn't set a personal best time in a long while, the recognition reinforces that their accomplishment matters."
>
> —Kevin Straughn

UNDERSTAND AND PRACTICE THE LEADERSHIP BEHAVIORS OF ENCOURAGE THE HEART

I encourage others as they work on activities and programs.

ENCOURAGE THE HEART

Reflect on Past Encouragements

Think about how you have encouraged others while they were working on something.

- What reactions did you observe from them?

- How did your encouragement impact the individual, group, or project?

Recall a time when you recognized someone on the spot for their actions.

- What was their reaction?

- How do you think this kind of immediate recognition would affect the group and the individual if done more frequently?

What are simple ways you can acknowledge someone during their work? What specific actions or behaviors should you look for to recognize someone effectively?

List five quick and simple ways to recognize someone in the moment. For example, give a verbal compliment.

1.

2.

3.

4.

5.

ENCOURAGE THE HEART

I express appreciation for the contributions people make.

Appreciating the People on Your Team

How can you show more appreciation for people's efforts? What common methods can you use to express gratitude? It's important to consider how best to show appreciation to the people on your team or in your group member.

List five ways you could show greater appreciation to someone in your group. Here's one example: publicly acknowledge an achievement in a meeting.

1.

2.

3.

4.

5.

How would individual members and the group as a whole benefit from more frequent expressions of appreciation?

How can you get better at "catching" people doing excellent work?

ENCOURAGE THE HEART

I make sure that people are creatively recognized for their contributions.

Send a Personal Message

Think of someone in your life whom you would like to send a specific, personal message to. This could be a friend, family member, teacher, mentor, or anyone else who has had a positive impact on your life. The message should be thoughtful, sincere, and reflect your genuine feelings or gratitude.

Reflect on the people in your life and choose someone who has made a difference to you or someone you appreciate.

Write a personal message to this person. Your message should include:

- A specific reason why you are thankful for them or why they are important to you

- An example of something they did that made an impact on you

- A positive wish or hope for them

Choose the best way to deliver your message. It could be through a handwritten note, an email, a text message, or even a phone call.

After you send your message, take some time to observe what happens next. Notice the response you receive and how it makes you feel. Reflect on the impact your words might have had on the recipient.

If you feel comfortable, share your experience with the class. Discuss how sending the message affected you and the recipient. What did you learn from this activity? How did it make you feel to express your gratitude or appreciation?

Reflection

- How did you choose the person to send your message to?

- What emotions did you experience while writing and sending the message?

- What response did you receive, and how did it make you feel?

- What did you learn about the power of personal communication?

ENCOURAGE THE HEART

I praise people for a job well done.

Name a time you were recognized for something you did.

- Describe your feelings and reactions when you were recognized. Did it change how you interacted with that group?

- How might others feel the same or differently from you when they are recognized?

Think of someone you saw in the past week doing something meaningful for a group you are in.

- Did you recognize that person?

- Why or why not?

- If not, how might you recognize them now?

In the past week, did you recognize anyone for something that affected the group? If yes, why did you decide to do that?

- What did you do, and why did you choose that approach?

If no, why not?

- Could you recognize that person now? If so, how would you do it?

- What difference would it make to recognize them now?

ENCOURAGE THE HEART

I make it a point to publicly recognize people who show commitment to shared values.

As a leader, consider how your group's values appear when demonstrated. For instance, what actions show integrity or other core values? By reflecting on this, you'll know what to look for when people show their commitment to the group's values.

Can you recall a recent example of someone in the group demonstrating the group's values?

- What did they do?

- How did you or the group acknowledge their actions?

- If they went unrecognized, what can you do differently next time?

Once you know what behavior aligns with the group's values, recognize it. Think about:

- When did the person demonstrate the value?

- What specifically did they do?

- Why does it matter to the group?

Reflect on an example from the first question or another experience and describe the when, what, and why approach you followed to recognize someone.

- When did the action happen?

- What did the person do?

- Why does it matter to the group?

ENCOURAGE THE HEART

I find ways for us to celebrate accomplishments.

Harry Potter and the Sorcerer's Stone (2002) Movie Activity

Professor Albus Dumbledore, the headmaster of Hogwarts, is winding down the school year and awarding the house cup to one of four residential houses based on a series of competitive events and other contributions to the school. In announcing the winner of the year's house cup, the professor describes a number of actions that members of one house took throughout the movie.

Watch this scene on YouTube from the movie "The House Cup - Harry Potter and the Philosopher's Stone": https://youtu.be/IGrvPFCQ6K8.

When you finish watching the clip, ask yourself these questions related to the scenes:

- What examples of Encourage the Heart did you see in this scene?

- What in the headmaster's remarks make them an example of Encourage the Heart? Is there anything he might have done differently?

- What was different about how the headmaster recognized each person? Were there examples of celebrating values in his remarks?

- After the remarks, what did you notice happening with everyone in the banquet hall?

"That experience taught me a lot. It taught me how much it meant to people to be found valuable for what they're good at and how much my experience as a success coach was about the relationship being a two-way street—the students I work with have a lot to teach me, too."

—Kadesha Zimmerman

FURTHER ACTIONS FOR INCREASING THE FREQUENCY OF ENCOURAGE THE HEART BEHAVIORS

Leadership development is an ongoing process. To continue improving as a leader, consider trying one or more of the following activities:

1. Publicly share stories about group members who have gone above and beyond. Highlight their exceptional contributions to the group.
2. During informal gatherings, take note of actions that embody the group's values. Acknowledge these contributions on the spot.
3. Write at least three thank-you notes each week to individuals who are positively affecting the group.
4. Find inexpensive, meaningful gifts to recognize and reward people. The thought and the story behind the gift matter more than the gift itself. Examples include photos, buttons, small stuffed animals, painted rocks, or ribbons.
5. During end-of-term or end-of-year activities, go beyond typical certificates or plaques. Share personal stories about individuals' extraordinary contributions to give greater meaning to their achievements.

CONNECT WHAT YOU LEARNED ABOUT ENCOURAGE THE HEART TO YOUR LEADERSHIP JOURNAL

The Leadership Journal is available on page 101 to help you shape your ongoing learning. After working through this Encourage the Heart section of the workbook and reviewing your Student Leadership Practices Inventory, we invite you capture some highlights of what you learned and consider your next steps. Use the journal section as a support tool for tackling your next leadership challenge.

8

My Leadership Journal

Your leadership development journey began when you read *The Student Leadership Challenge*, completed The Student Leadership Practices Inventory, and started working your way through this workbook. But it doesn't end there! This Leadership Journal is intended to support your ongoing leadership development journey.

Research tells us that becoming a better leader does not magically happen after attending a single workshop or class. It's an ongoing process, one that requires deliberate practice. That practice is most effective when you take time to reflect on what you've learned and then try again. This journal is designed to encourage that repeatable process.

The sections in this Leadership Journal are organized into five parts:

1. **Review** Your LPI Data
2. **Identify** Your Next Leadership Challenge
3. **Map** Your Approach
4. **Act** on Your Plan
5. **Reflect** on Your Progress

> "The key to leadership is being intentional. . . . I found out that learning goes side by side with knowing who I was as a person and as a leader."
>
> —Tarek Aly

STEP 1. REVIEW YOUR LPI DATA

Practice Ranking

Review your Student LPI report and in the following table rank the frequency you demonstrate each practice and note the one practice you do most frequently. After you have identified the practice(s) you do most frequently, make some notes about opportunities you anticipate for further demonstrating each of the practices.

Practice and Commitments	Frequency Ranking
Model the Way	
Inspire a Shared Vision	
Challenge the Process	
Enable Others to Act	
Encourage the Heart	

BUILD ON YOUR STRENGTHS

Now that you have completed the activities in this workbook what additional opportunities do you see to continue demonstrating The Five Practices? You can identify opportunities you see arising in the next week or two and any longer-term opportunities.

STEP 2. YOUR LPI DATA

Review the thirty leadership behaviors that make up your Student LPI report. Using this table, you can make notes of your observations and what you learned after completing the workbook activities. Add check marks and/or circle the ones you want to note or use highlighters to organize or prioritize them. Think about which behaviors you will prioritize as you continue your leadership development journey.

(**Note:** the six behaviors are listed in the order that they appear in your Student LPI report. This differs from the order they appear in the practice sections of this workbook.)

Practice	Observations and Notes
Model the Way	
I set a personal example of what I expect from other people.	
I spend time making sure that people behave consistently with the principles and standards we have agreed on.	
I follow through on the promises and commitments I make.	
I seek to understand how my actions affect other people's performance.	
I make sure that people support the values we have agreed on.	
I talk about my values and the principles that guide my actions.	
Inspire a Shared Vision	
I look ahead and communicate what I believe will affect us in the future.	
I describe to others in our organization what we should be capable of accomplishing.	
I talk with others about a vision of how things could be even better in the future.	

Practice	Observations and Notes
I talk with others about how their own interests can be met by working toward a common goal.	
I am upbeat and positive when talking about what we can accomplish.	
I speak with passion about the higher purpose and meaning of what we are doing.	
Challenge the Process	
I look for ways to develop and challenge my skills and abilities.	
I look for ways that others can try out new ideas and methods.	
I search for innovative ways to improve what we are doing.	
When things don't go as we expected, I ask, "What can we learn from this experience?"	
I make sure that big projects we undertake are broken down into smaller and doable parts.	
I take initiative in experimenting with the way things can be done.	
Enable Others to Act	
I foster cooperative rather than competitive relationships among people I work with.	
I actively listen to diverse points of view.	
I treat others with dignity and respect.	
I support the decisions that other people make on their own.	
I give others a great deal of freedom and choice in deciding how to do their work.	
I provide opportunities for others to take on leadership responsibilities.	

(Continued)

(Continued)

Practice	Observations and Notes
Encourage the Heart	
I praise people for a job well done.	
I encourage others as they work on activities and programs.	
I express appreciation for the contributions that people make.	
I make it a point to publicly recognize people who show commitment to shared values.	
I find ways for us to celebrate accomplishments.	
I make sure that people are creatively recognized for their contributions.	

Your ***LPI Data*** Wrap-Up

Now that you've made your way through the workbook and reviewed your Student LPI data, which three behaviors do you want to continue practicing? Describe your plan to continue practicing these behaviors?

Behavior	How Will You Increase the Frequency of the Behavior?

CONTINUING YOUR LEADERSHIP DEVELOPMENT JOURNEY

There is no substitute for learning by doing. The more frequently you demonstrate the leadership behaviors, the greater the possibility you will achieve extraordinary results. It is in the doing that you discover your potential to engage others in meaningful progress. Use this Leadership Journal to define the actions you will take to define and tackle your next leadership challenge.

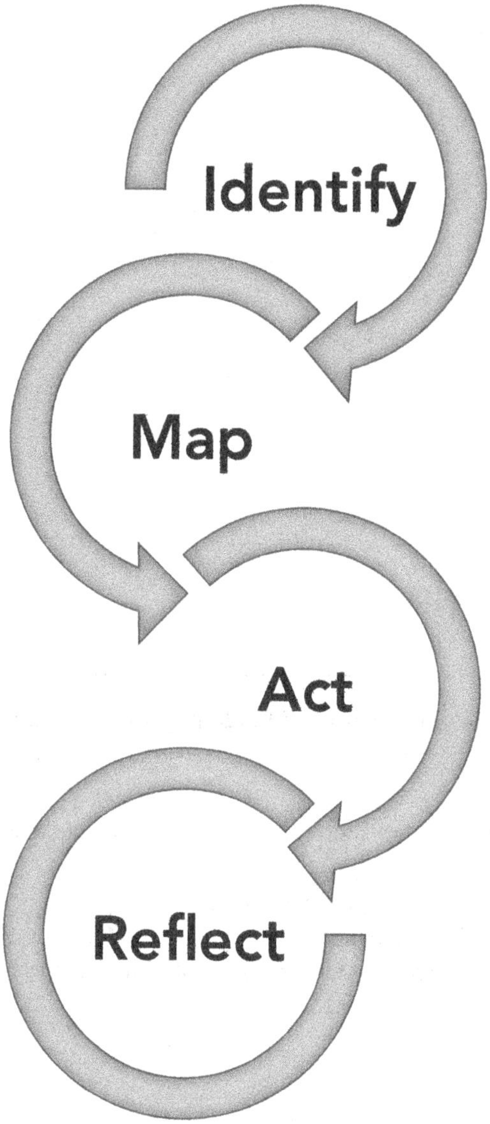

Identify Your Next Leadership Challenge

What leadership challenge do you want to take on next? Here are some ideas to consider:

- I want to move from being a member of a group or team to serving as an officer or captain.
- I want to become an excellent public speaker.
- I want to start a club that is dedicated to taking action against climate change.

My Next Challenge:

Think about what else you might need to identify, define, and prepare for your next challenge.

- Do you need to gather more information to fully understand the issue before moving forward?
- Do you need to ask for input from others?
- Do you have other obligations that you need to finish or offload before you will have enough time and mental energy to fully embrace this challenge?

Identify Your Next Leadership Challenge Wrap-Up

Now that you have identified your next leadership challenge, reflect on your current skills and the context of your challenge.

Identify areas where your leadership skills could be further developed or where there are significant opportunities for personal growth that would help with this challenge.
What is getting in the way of completing this challenge?

MAP YOUR APPROACH

A good way to map your approach is by committing to S.M.A.R.T. actions. This acronym stands for specific, measurable, attainable, realistic, and timely. By following the S.M.A.R.T. criteria, you can map your approach by creating actionable steps toward enhancing your leadership capabilities, leading to tangible improvements over time. Identifying S.M.A.R.T. actions can greatly increase the likelihood that you will keep your commitment.

Here are some ideas for applying S.M.A.R.T. criteria to your leadership development:

Specific. Define a specific aspect of leadership you want to develop. For example, "Enhance communication skills to effectively articulate ideas and inspire team members."

Measurable. Determine how you will measure progress. This could involve tracking the number of presentations given, receiving feedback from peers, or observing improvements in team collaboration.

Attainable. Ensure that your goal is realistic and feasible given your current abilities and resources. Consider the time and effort required for training, practice, and feedback.

Realistic. Set a goal that is challenging but within reach. It should push you out of your comfort zone but still be achievable with dedication and effort.

Timely. Establish a timeline for achieving your leadership development goal. For instance, "Improve communication skills through regular practice and feedback sessions over the next six months."

By following the S.M.A.R.T. criteria, you can create actionable steps toward enhancing your leadership capabilities, leading to tangible improvements over time. Use this table to jot down some initial ideas, and then refine them on the next page.

Specific
Measurable
Attainable
Realistic
Timely

My Next Leadership Challenge:
My SMART Approach

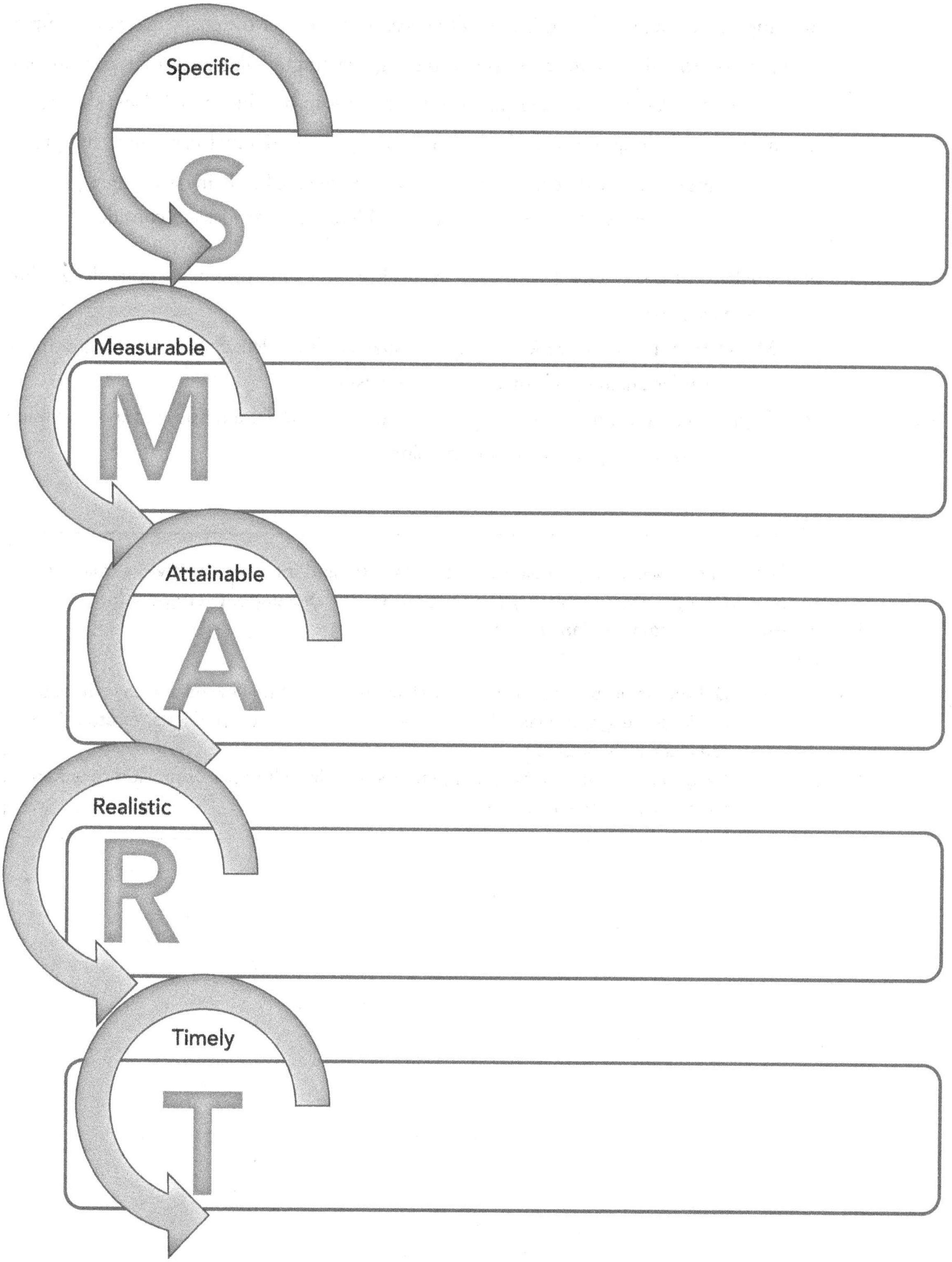

ACT ON YOUR PLAN

Achieving the extraordinary is rarely easy. It's not called a leadership challenge for nothing. Achieving small wins is one of the best ways to meet the challenge. For example, a soccer player who wants to improve their game might take time to focus on one particular skill. Perhaps they dedicate several practices to building speed. Next they focus on improving their agility with the ball. Practicing the individual parts gives the player a targeted improvement that aligns with the long-range goal of being a stronger player.

How do you next want to act on your plan? Here are some ideas to consider:

- Feedback. I want to use feedback to make continuous improvements in my leadership challenge approach.
- Mentorship. I want to work with my personal coach to identify how I can better mentor my student mentees on diversity and inclusion.
- Teamwork. I want to recruit a group of individuals who are passionate about climate change and can help me define our mission.

Think about what ways you can demonstrate and practice behaviors that will strengthen your leadership capacity related to this challenge. Every goal for tomorrow requires some actions today.

- Did you dedicate time each week to learning something new related to your leadership challenge, perhaps through books, online courses, podcasts, or attending seminars and workshops?
- Did you act on having the courage to address difficult topics or provide constructive feedback when necessary?

Act on Your Plan Wrap-Up

Now that you have a strategy for acting on your plan, what are some ways you can do the following:

Implement your plan of action systematically.
Delegate tasks as necessary and monitor progress closely.
Stay flexible and adapt your approach as needed based on feedback and changing circumstances.

REFLECT ON YOUR PROGRESS

How is it going? Think about what you have learned and practiced. What will you do next based on this experience?

Take time to reflect on and complete these phrases based on your experience so far.

This is what went well:
This is what didn't go so well:

Reflect on Your Progress Wrap-Up

How has what you have learned about leadership helped you with your leadership challenge?

Which of the thirty behaviors have you used in your leadership challenge plan so far?
Which of the thirty behaviors do you plan to use as you continue to make progress?

Congratulations! By working through these prompts, you have continued your learning about leadership and how to achieve extraordinary results. Keep in mind that this a repeatable process, so please refer to these pages again when you are ready to take on your next leadership challenge!

9

Ten Tips for Becoming a Better Leader

You've made an excellent start on your journey to becoming a better leader! We applaud your dedication and commitment. As you continue on this path, we'd like to leave you with some learning and practice tips that will help you on your way.

1. BE SELF-AWARE

The best leaders are highly aware of what's going on inside of them as they are leading. They're also very aware of the impact they're having on others. Think about it this way. Let's say you start falling behind in a class. You tell yourself you can catch up easily, so you ignore a couple of low grades on spot quizzes. Then one day you realize that the midterm is coming up and you haven't cracked a book in weeks. You ignored the work for so long it's going to cost you a lot in terms of time and grades.

The same is true in leading. Self-awareness gives you clues about what's going on inside you and in your environment. If you ignore those clues, you might find it difficult or impossible to catch up.

Your feelings are messages that are trying to teach you something. So, listen and learn, take time to reflect on your experiences, and keep a journal. As you go through your developmental experiences, look within yourself and pay attention to how you're feeling.

2. MANAGE YOUR EMOTIONS

The best leaders are careful not to let their feelings manage them. Instead, they manage their feelings.

Let's say that you tend to get angry when people come unprepared for a meeting. You could express your anger and put them down in front of the group. But would that be the best way to handle the situation? Common sense says that it wouldn't. The better choice would be to be aware of your anger, acknowledge it, and then decide on the most effective way to deal with the problem. The same is true in learning.

Sometimes you will feel frustrated and upset by the feedback that you receive. You might even feel angry at the person who gave you the feedback. Be aware of your feelings, but don't let them rule your behavior. If you sense that you need help managing your emotions, seek it from a trusted teacher, advisor, counselor, family member, or cleric.

3. SEEK FEEDBACK

The best leaders ask for feedback from others—feedback not only about what they're doing well but also about what they're not doing well. Let people know that you genuinely want their feedback, and then do something with the feedback they give you. Afterward, ask, "How'd I do?" Have a conversation. Then say thanks.

4. TAKE THE INITIATIVE

The Leadership Challenge research is clear on this point: the best leaders don't wait for someone else to tell them what to do. They take the initiative to find and solve problems and to meet and create challenges. The same is true in learning: the best leaders take charge of their own learning. Because they're self-aware and seek feedback, they know their strengths and weaknesses, and they know what they need to learn. They find a way to get the experience, example, or education they need. It's your learning, your life. Take charge of it.

5. SEEK HELP

Top athletes, musicians, and performing artists all have coaches. Leadership is a performing art, too, and it never hurts to have some help. Ask a teacher, group advisor, or mentor you respect to watch you perform, give you feedback, offer suggestions for improvement, and give you support generally. You can also consider fellow students and friends whom you feel have great leadership experiences. If you are employed, consider a coworker or supervisor. You might find yourself working with a couple of coaches who have expertise in different areas you want to explore.

6. SET GOALS AND MAKE A PLAN

If you have a clear sense of what you want to accomplish, you'll be much more likely to apply what you learn. Leaders who are successful at bringing out the best in themselves and in others set achievable stretch goals—goals that are high but not so far out of reach that people give up even before they start.

It's also important to make your goals public. You will work harder to improve when you've told others what you're trying to accomplish.

Once you've set goals, make a plan. There may be several ways to get from where you are to where you want to be, just as there are several routes you could take to travel across the country. Pick the one that best suits your needs.

When you make your plan, remember that journeys are completed one step at a time. It's the same with leadership development. Take it step-by-step. There is no such thing as overnight success in becoming an exemplary leader.

7. PRACTICE, PRACTICE, PRACTICE

People who practice often are more likely to become experts at what they do than those who don't practice. We know this is true in the arts and in sports, but the same idea hasn't always been applied to leadership.

Practice is essential to learning. Practice might be rehearsing a speech or a new way of running a meeting. It might be sitting down with a friend to try out a conversation you plan to have with a member of your group.

Whatever it is, practice gives you the chance to become comfortable with and try out new methods, behaviors, and strategies in a safe environment. In fact, every experience is a form of practice, even when it's for real. Whether the experience is a raving success or a miserable failure, ask yourself and those involved, "What went well? What went poorly?" "What did I do well? What did I do poorly?" "What could I improve?" The best leaders are the best learners, and learning can occur at anytime and anywhere.

8. MEASURE PROGRESS

Measuring progress is crucial to improvement no matter what the activity—strengthening endurance, increasing speed, or becoming a better leader. The best measurement systems are ones that are visible and instant—like the speedometer on your dashboard or the watch on your wrist. For instance, you can count how many thank-you notes you send out by keeping a log. A self-monitoring system can include asking for feedback. Another way to monitor your progress is to retake the Student LPI.

9. REWARD YOURSELF

Connect your performance to rewards. It's nice when others recognize you for your efforts, but that doesn't always happen. So along with the goals that you set and the measurement system that you put in place, create some ways to reward yourself for achieving your goals. Give yourself a night off to go to a movie or a party with a friend. Buy yourself something you'd like; it doesn't have to be expensive. Mark the achievement in red pen on your calendar.

10. BE HONEST WITH YOURSELF AND HUMBLE WITH OTHERS

We know from The Leadership Challenge research that credibility is the foundation of leadership and honesty is at the top of the list of what constituents look for in a leader.

But what does honesty have to do with learning to lead? Everything. The ongoing research has yet to produce a leader with a perfect Student LPI score. Everyone can improve, and the first step is understanding, and acknowledging, what needs improving.

Being honest means that you're willing to admit mistakes, own up to your faults, and be open to suggestions for improvement. It also means that you're accepting of the same in others.

Being honest with yourself and others produces a level of humility that earns you credibility. People don't respect know-it-alls, especially when the know-it-all doesn't know it all. Admitting mistakes and being open to new ideas and new learning communicates that you are willing to grow. It promotes a culture of honesty and openness that's healthy for you and for others.

Hubris, that is, excessive pride, is the killer disease in leadership. It's fun to be a leader, gratifying to have influence, and exhilarating when people cheer your every word. But it's easy to be seduced by power and importance. Humility is the only way to resolve the conflicts and contradictions of leadership. Excessive pride can be avoided only if you recognize that you're human and need the help of others.

Final Thoughts as You Continue Your Leadership Journey

Congratulations for navigating your way through this workbook! However far you made it through the many suggestions, activities, and reflections, we hope you feel good about your progress toward becoming a better leader. We've tried to make leadership simple to understand and show what it looks like in practice, but simple doesn't mean that it is easy to be a leader or to learn how to become an even better leader.

No one is perfect. Every leader has flaws, and no one gets it right the first time or even every time. In sports, we see how professionals make the difficult look easy and how amateurs make the easy look difficult. Being professional is an ongoing endeavor no matter the sport, the setting, or the situation. Being a leader is no different. Despite your best efforts and most noble intentions, things won't always work out as you hoped, people will not always do what they promised or are capable of, and forces beyond your control will derail your plans.

Perhaps the truest test of leadership is in people's ability to bounce back from defeat and adversity, to pick themselves up and try again. History shows us that this quality of resilience is characteristic of all great leaders, and deeper analyses show that this stems from their being both clear and committed to a set of values and way of being. Becoming a better leader, as we indicated at the onset, begins with clarifying your values, finding your voice, and conscientiously aligning your actions with shared values.

You make a difference. Don't let anyone or anything that happens persuade you otherwise. You'll be amazed by how many opportunities you have every day to act as a leader and make a difference. And you'll be pleasantly surprised by how much improvement you will be able to make by being more conscientious and intentional about acting as a leader.

Acknowledgments

Of all the leadership lessons we have learned over the years, the one that most needs repeating is this one: "You can't do it alone." Leadership is not a solo performance; it's a collaborative effort. And so is writing, editing, and producing a guide like this one. We—Jim, Barry, Lisa, and June—couldn't have done this without the expertise, dedication, and caring of the wonderful team of exceptional people who made this possible. Each and every one of you played a crucial role in this journey, and we are deeply grateful for your contributions.

First, the creation of *The Student Leadership Challenge: Student Workbook and Leadership Journal, Fourth Edition* is due to of the gracious support of our good colleagues in colleges, universities, secondary schools, and community organizations who have dedicated themselves to developing emerging leaders. Their commitment to student leadership is inspiring, and their acceptance of our research, content, and methods has indeed encouraged our hearts. We gratefully acknowledge the administrators, educators, and students who contributed their creative ideas and personal stories to this guide and our understanding of leadership dynamics in their settings.

We've enjoyed a four-decades-long partnership with our publisher, John Wiley & Sons. We've been a team since the beginning, and it's always a great joy to collaborate with them. We are deeply grateful for their continued support and belief in our work. Their unwavering support has been instrumental in bringing this guide to life, and we couldn't have done it without you.

A very loud shout-out goes to our editor, Amy Fandrei. Amy has been the champion of all *The Student Leadership Challenge* materials, continuously encouraging and driving us to improve how we present our work. Amy made this revised edition happen, and she has been our guiding star on this project. Thanks also to Sophie Thompson, editorial assistant, for keeping us on track in completing the manuscript; Tricia Weinhold, our senior brand manager, for fostering collaboration between the student and professional publications within *The Leadership Challenge* brand; and Pete Gaughan, senior managing editor, for guiding the process from manuscript submission through book publication.

At the beginning of each day when we begin our work and at the end of the day when we shut down the computer for a little rest, our families are there to share their love and support. We are blessed with their generous encouragement, helpful feedback, and constructive coaching. Their presence and understanding have been instrumental in our creative process. To our families, we want to express our deepest gratitude for your unwavering support and understanding. You are our rock and we couldn't have done this without you.

Jim and Barry are lucky to have extraordinary partners in Tae Kouzes and Jackie Schmidt-Posner. They are also blessed with the inspiration and perspective of their children. High fives and big hugs for Nicholas Lopez, Jim's stepson; Kimberly Lopez, Jim's daughter-in-law; and Amanda Posner and Darryl Collins, Barry's daughter and son-in-law.

With all these very special people in our lives, it highlights how true it is that leadership is an affair of the heart.

About the Authors

Jim Kouzes and **Barry Posner** have been working together for more than forty years, studying leaders, researching leadership, conducting leadership development seminars, and providing leadership in various capacities, with and without titles. They are coauthors of the award-winning, best-selling book *The Leadership Challenge*, which has sold more than three million copies worldwide and is available in more than twenty-two languages. It has won numerous awards, including the Critics' Choice Award from the nation's book review editors and book-of-the-year awards from the American Council of Healthcare Executives and Fast Company. *The Leadership Challenge* is listed in *The Top 100 Business Books of All Time* as one of the Top 10 books on leadership. *The Student Leadership Challenge: Five Practices for Becoming an Exemplary Leader* has become a standard leadership development book and resource for young people and students from middle to high school, undergraduate to graduate levels. More than 500 colleges and universities use *The Student Leadership Challenge* and *The Student Leadership Practices Inventory* in their classes, seminars, programs, and workshops.

Jim and Barry have coauthored more than a dozen other award-winning leadership books, including these titles:

- *Everyday People*
- *Extraordinary Leadership*
- *Leadership in Higher Education*
- *Stop Selling & Start Leading*
- *Learning Leadership*
- *The Five Fundamentals for Becoming an Exemplary Leader*
- *Turning Adversity into Opportunity*
- *Finding the Courage to Lead*
- *Great Leadership Creates Great Workplaces*
- *Credibility: How Leaders Gain and Lose It, Why People Demand It*
- *The Truth About Leadership: The No-Fads, Heart-of-the-Matter Facts You Need to Know*

- *Encouraging the Heart: A Leader's Guide to Recognizing and Rewarding Others*
- *A Leader's Legacy, Extraordinary Leadership in Australia and New Zealand*
- *Making Extraordinary Things Happen in Asia*

Jim and Barry developed the widely used and highly acclaimed *LPI®: Leadership Practices Inventory* and *The Student Leadership Practices Inventory (S-LPI)*. These 360-degree questionnaires provide insights into how frequently leaders use empirically identified behaviors as essential to bringing out the best in people and teams. Worldwide, nearly one million students have completed the Student LPI, and more than five million people have taken the LPI. Over a thousand research studies around the globe have been based on The Five Practices of Exemplary Leadership® framework. More information about these books, inventories, and studies is available at www.leadershipchallenge.com.

Among the honors and awards that Jim and Barry have received are highest award from the Association for Talent and Development (ATD) for their Distinguished Contribution to Workplace Learning and Performance, named Management/Leadership Educators of the Year by the International Management Council, ranked by *Leadership Excellence* magazine in the top 20 on their list of the Top 100 Thought Leaders, named by Coaching for Leadership in the Top 50 Leadership Coaches in the nation, considered by *HR Magazine* as one of the Most Influential International Thinkers, and, listed among the Top 75 Management Experts in the *World by Inc.* magazine.

Jim and Barry are frequent keynote speakers, and each has conducted leadership development programs for hundreds of organizations, including Apple, Applied Materials, ARCO, AT&T, Australia Institute of Management, Australia Post, Bank of America, Bose, Charles Schwab, Cisco Systems, Clorox, Community Leadership Association, Conference Board of Canada, Consumers Energy, Deloitte Touche, Dow Chemical, Egon Zehnder International, Federal Express, Genentech, Google, Gymboree, Hewlett-Packard, IBM, Jobs DR-Singapore, Johnson & Johnson, Kaiser Foundation Health Plans and Hospitals, Intel, Itaú Unibanco, L.L.Bean, Lawrence Livermore National Labs, Lucile Packard Children's Hospital, Merck, Motorola, NetApp, Northrop Grumman, Novartis, Oakwood Housing, Oracle, Petronas, Roche Bioscience, Siemens, 3M, Topgolf/Callaway Brands, Toyota, U.S. Postal Service, United Way, USAA, Verizon, VISA, Westpac, and the Walt Disney Company. In addition, they have presented seminars and lectures at well over one hundred college and university campuses.

Jim Kouzes is a fellow at the Doerr Institute for New Leaders at Rice University and has been the Dean's Executive Fellow of Leadership at the Leavey School of Business, Santa Clara University. He lectures on leadership worldwide to corporations, governments, and nonprofits. He is a highly regarded leadership scholar and an experienced executive. *The Wall Street Journal* hailed him as one of the twelve best executive educators in the United States. Jim has received the Thought Leadership Award from the Instructional Systems Association, the most prestigious award given by the trade association of training and development industry providers, and the Golden Gavel, the highest honor awarded by Toastmasters International.

Jim served as president, CEO, and chairman of the Tom Peters Company for eleven years, and led the Executive Development Center at Santa Clara University for seven years. He was the founder and executive director for eight years of the Joint Center for Human Services Development at San Jose State University and was on the staff of the School of Social Work, University of Texas. His career in training and development began in 1969 when he conducted seminars for Community Action Agency staff and volunteers in the war on poverty. Following graduation from Michigan State University (BA with honors in political science), he served as a Peace Corps volunteer (1967–1969). You can reach Jim directly at jim@kouzes.com.

Barry Posner chairs the Management and Entrepreneurship Department at the Leavey School of Business, Santa Clara University, where he previously served for six years as associate dean for graduate education, six years as associate dean for executive education, and twelve years as dean of the School. He holds the Michael J. Accolti, S.J. Professorship, teaching leadership courses for both undergraduate and graduate students. He has been a distinguished visiting professor around the globe: Hong Kong University of Science and Technology, Sabanci University (Istanbul), University of Western Australia, University of Auckland (New Zealand), and Seattle University.

At Santa Clara, Barry has received the President's Distinguished Faculty Award, the Leavey School's Extraordinary Faculty Award, and several other outstanding teaching and academic honors. An internationally renowned scholar and educator, he is the author or coauthor of more than one hundred research and practitioner-focused articles. He serves on the editorial review board for the *Leadership & Organizational Development Journal, Journal of Business Ethics, Administrative Sciences*, and *Frontiers in Psychology*.

Barry received his baccalaureate degree with honors in political science from the University of California, Santa Barbara; his master's degree in public administration from The Ohio State University; and his doctoral degree in organizational behavior and administrative theory from the University of Massachusetts, Amherst. Having consulted worldwide with many public and private sector organizations, he also works strategically with several community-based and professional organizations. He has served previously on the board of the American Institute of Architects (AIA), Big Brothers/Big Sisters of Santa Clara County, Center for Excellence in Nonprofits, Junior Achievement of Silicon Valley and Monterey Bay, Public Allies, San Jose Repertory Theatre, SVCreates, Sigma Phi Epsilon Fraternity, Uplift Family Services, and several start-up companies. Barry can be reached at bposner@scu.edu.